GREAT MOMENTS IN OLYMPIC HISTORY

Olympic Wrestling

Barbara M. Linde

rosen publishing's
rosen
central®

New York

To my parents, Richard and Doris Linde, who encouraged my love of reading.

Published in 2007 by The Rosen Publishing Group, Inc.
29 East 21st Street, New York, NY 10010

First Edition

Library of Congress Cataloging-in-Publication Data

Linde, Barbara M.
  Olympic wrestling / Barbara M. Linde.
      p. cm. – (Great moments in Olympic history)
  Includes bibliographical references and index.
  ISBN-13: 978-1-4042-0972-5
  ISBN-10: 1-4042-0972-7 (library binding)
  1. Wrestling—History—Juvenile literature. 2. Olympics—History—Juvenile literature.
I. Title.
  GV1195.3.L56 2007
  796.812–dc22

                                    2006033445

Manufactured in the United States of America

On the cover: Rulon Gardner celebrates his bronze medal at the 2004 Summer Olympics in Athens, Greece. Gardner achieved this victory in spite of injuries that could have ended his career.

CONTENTS

CHAPTER 1

A Brief History of the Olympic Games

The original Olympic Games began in ancient Greece in 776 B.C. By that time, wrestling was already ancient. Many historians believe wrestling is the world's oldest competitive sport. They've found images of wrestlers on Egyptian wall paintings that are 5,000 years old. Wrestlers also appear on ancient Greek vases and in old stories and myths.

Some Greek myths say the god Zeus wrestled his father, Kronos, for control of the world and won. To celebrate, Zeus held athletic contests for the gods at a place called Olympia, which is in the city-state of Elis in western Greece. Over time, Olympia became an important religious center. Many people came there to honor Zeus; his wife, Hera; and ancient heroes.

Olympic Myths

An ancient Greek poet named Pindar wrote that the hero Herakles (Hercules) created the first Olympics after he completed one of his labors—cleaning the horse stables that belonged to King Augeas. These games were held at Olympia.

Another story credited Greek hero Theseus with creating the rules of wrestling. Before him, wrestling had been simply a rough fight in which only size and strength mattered. Theseus made wrestling a sport with specific moves.

The Ancient Olympics

Around 776 B.C., King Iphitos of Elis became concerned about a plague in the country, as well as the continuing wars between the city-states. He asked advice from the oracle at Delphi, a highly respected priestess who predicted the future. The oracle told King Iphitos to honor Zeus with athletic games at Olympia.

The king arranged for a truce among Greek city-states so athletes and spectators could travel safely to Olympia. The first Olympic Games had only one event, a footrace called the *stade* or *stadion*. A local athlete named Koroibos won. Legends say the plague ended and there was peace for a while. For many centuries, the Olympic Games were held at Olympia every 4 years.

Residents of Elis worked as committee members, judges, and trainers. Over time, more than twenty-four marble buildings and tracks were built at Olympia.

Think of Olympia as a religious center and sports complex

combined. There were temples and altars to Zeus, Hera, and ancient heroes, as well as other gods and goddesses. Athletes had a stadium, buildings to practice in, and outdoor tracks. People went there to pray and see the Olympics, but no one lived there.

The Olympic Games were held 293 times over the next 1,200 years. They became wildly popular, and the number of athletes, events, and spectators grew steadily over time. Records show that by 150 B.C., about 40,000 spectators attended the games.

The End of the Ancient Olympics

In 146 B.C., the Roman Empire conquered Greece. At first, the Romans let the Olympic Games continue. Romans participated and even held similar games in other countries of their empire. But in A.D. 393, the Roman emperor Theodosius I, who was a Christian, ended the Olympic Games because of their pagan nature.

Olympia slowly disappeared. Roman rulers used parts of the Olympic buildings for their own projects. Earthquakes and floods buried Olympia's remains under mounds of dirt and mud. The ruins were mostly forgotten. Then an amateur archaeologist redis-covered them around 1766. Archaeologists began to uncover them in 1826 and piece together the story of the ancient Olympics.

The Modern Olympics

In the late 1800s, a Frenchman named Pierre de Coubertin became interested in the ancient Olympics. Coubertin thought,

Women and the Ancient Olympics

The Greeks did not allow women to compete in the Olympics. Only single women could attend the games; married women could be put to death if they were caught watching them. A woman named Kallipateira took this risk to watch her son compete. She disguised herself as a trainer. When her son won, she leapt into the arena, losing her clothes in the process. People realized she was a woman! Since she came from a famous Olympic family, she was not killed. After that, however, trainers—like athletes—were not allowed to wear clothes.

much as King Iphitos of Elis had, that the games could help promote world peace. Athletes from all over the world would compete for medals, but not for money.

The wealthy Coubertin used a lot of his money to promote his idea. Others offered more financing. In 1896, 241 male athletes from fourteen countries attended the first modern Olympics in Athens, Greece. They competed in forty-three events, including wrestling.

The games have been held on a regular basis since 1896. However, no games were held in 1916 because of World War I, or in 1940 and 1944 because of World War II.

The Olympic Flame that is lit at the beginning of each modern Olympics starts its journey to the site of the modern games here in the ruins of ancient Olympia. It is then carried by a series of runners until it finally arrives at the site of that year's games

Baron Pierre de Coubertin was born in 1863 and died in 1937. Without his persistence and financial support, the modern Olympics might not exist.

Did You Know?

Baron Pierre de Coubertin was a French educator. In the late 1800s, he encouraged adding athletics to the French education system as a way to help build character. The archaeological discoveries in ancient Greece inspired him to promote international athletic competitions. In 1894, he organized the International Congress on Amateurism. The experts at that meeting established the International Olympic Committee (IOC). Coubertin became the first secretary general of the IOC. As a result of his work, he was nominated for the Nobel Peace Prize in 1936.

New games, such as basketball and volleyball, have been added over the years. Beginning in 1900, women were allowed to compete. Now there are both Summer and Winter Games. Unlike the ancient games, which were always held at Olympia, the modern games travel all over the world. Countries that have hosted the Olympics include the United States, Australia, France, Sweden, Japan, Mexico, South Korea, Canada, and—for the 2008 Summer Games—China.

Later you'll read more about the achievements of ancient wrestlers such as Eurybatus, Hipposthenes, and Milo of Croton. You'll also learn about accomplishments of modern wrestlers such as George Mehnert, Carl Westergren, Ivar Johansson, Aleksandr Medved, Aleksandr Karelin, Rulon Gardner, Irini Merleni, Kaori Icho, and Wang Xu. But first, let's see what it was like to attend the ancient games!

In early April 1896, spectators poured into the restored Olympic stadium in Athens, Greece, to attend the first modern Olympics.

CHAPTER 2

A Look at the Ancient Olympics

The Olympics in 776 B.C. lasted only 1 day and included only one event, the *stade* or *stadion*. As more events were added, the ancient games came to last 5 days. These games were highly organized, with specific events and activities scheduled for each day.

The ancient games were held at the time of the second or third full moon after the summer solstice. According to the calendar we use today, that would mean they took place during the extreme heat of mid-August or mid-September.

People came from all over the Greek empire to watch the games. Many spectators set up tents or more elaborate pavilions around Olympia. Others slept on the ground in the open. Travelers brought some food with them and could also buy food at the games.

Instructions for the Athletes

Wrestlers, like all the athletes, heard these words from the judges: "If you have worked in a manner worthy of coming to Olympia, and have done nothing in an offhand or base way, proceed with good courage; but as for those who have not so exercised, go away wherever you like."

The First Day

The ancient Olympics began with a swearing-in ceremony. The athletes, their fathers and brothers, and the trainers and judges took an oath to follow the rules. The athletes promised they were freeborn Greeks, since slaves and foreigners could not compete. Each athlete also swore he had trained for 10 months. All agreed not to cheat or take bribes. The judges promised to be fair.

Boys from ages 12 to 18 had their running, wrestling, and boxing contests on the first day. In the afternoon, athletes and spectators visited with each other, prayed, or saw the sights at Olympia.

The Second Day

The second day began with a parade of horses, riders, and chariots. Horse and chariot races took place on a large oval track called the hippodrome, from the Greek words for "horse" and "racecourse." Later in the day, the pentathlon was held. This event had five contests, in this order: discus throw, javelin throw, jumping, running, and wrestling. If one athlete won the first three contests, the last two were eliminated.

The Third Day

The third day started with a solemn religious ritual. The athletes and judges, along with important officials from the different Greek city-states, had a procession. They took food and drinks in gold and silver containers to Zeus's temple as an offering.

Runners had races of varying lengths in the afternoon. There was a banquet in the evening for all the athletes, their families, and the spectators.

The Fourth Day

The contact sports of wrestling, boxing, and the *pankration*—a combination of wrestling and boxing—happened on the fourth day, as did running in armor. The three contact sports took place in the stadium. They were known as combat sports because the skills required were important skills for soldiers. Most Greek men were trained from boyhood to serve as soldiers, so they were

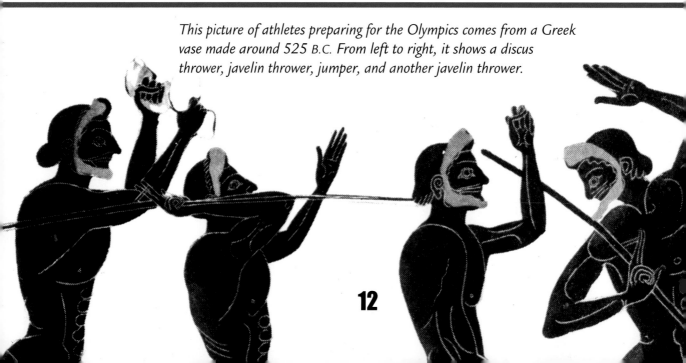

This picture of athletes preparing for the Olympics comes from a Greek vase made around 525 B.C. From left to right, it shows a discus thrower, javelin thrower, jumper, and another javelin thrower.

familiar with the skills for these events.

The contact sports held many dangers for athletes. There weren't many rules, and athletes were encouraged to be aggressive. Sometimes athletes killed their opponents—and went unpunished!

Wrestling was the first event of the day, and it was one of the most popular ancient Olympic sports. Boxing was next. Boxers wore leather strips wrapped around their hands rather than the padded gloves used today. The matches had no time limits, so competitors fought until one gave up, was knocked out, or died.

The most violent combat sport was the *pankration*, which means "all powerful" or "all strong." This contest was brutal, vicious—and wildly popular. Because competitors threw each other to the ground, the stadium's hard dirt surface was turned into a sticky mud the Greeks called "beeswax." Two athletes hit, kicked, punched, and choked each other. They struck without mercy at every part of the body, often injuring and sometimes killing an opponent. The contest went on until one athlete raised a finger to signal defeat.

The race in armor, also called the *hoplitodromos*, finished the fourth day. The racers wore soldiers' heavy armor and carried large round shields. The race reminded Greek citizens that one purpose of athletics was to prepare men for battle. The *hoplitodro-*

mos could also be amusing, as racers tried to gather speed and look graceful while being weighed down with armor.

The Fifth Day

The final day was a time for celebrations. No events were held. Instead, the athletes, trainers, and spectators walked to the Temple of Zeus, led by the winners. The winners wore purple ribbons around their heads and arms as marks of their victories. Once everyone reached the temple, the judges presented crowns made from the branches of a sacred olive tree to the winners. These were the only rewards the winners received at the games! Banquets and parties filled the rest of the day and most of the night.

The winners received abundant rewards when they returned

Today, this is all that remains of the once splendid Temple of Zeus at Olympia. In ancient times, it held one of the Seven Wonders of the Ancient World—a gold and ivory statue of Zeus that was about 40 feet (12 m) tall.

home. For most of them, there were victory parades, banquets, and such valuable gifts as money, houses, and chariots. An Olympic winner was usually guaranteed an excellent way of life until his death.

Sadly, athletes who did not win were not treated well. The ancient Greek poet Pindar wrote that losers used less-traveled back roads to return home and often hid from others along the way and once they were home. In a society that valued victory and strength, losing athletes were dishonored and ashamed. In spite of this, athletes flocked to Olympia every 4 years for their chance at victory.

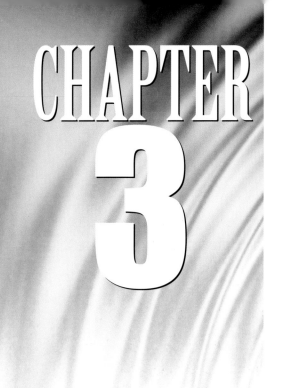

CHAPTER 3

Ancient Olympic Wrestling

Wrestling became an Olympic sport in 708 B.C. and was soon the most popular sport. Most Greek men—and in Sparta, women as well—engaged in wrestling as a sport. However, only the best male wrestlers tried out for the Olympics.

What Did It Take to Win?

Here's what an ancient Greek writer said athletes needed to do in order to train for the Olympics:

You will have to obey instructions, eat according to regulations, keep away from desserts, exercise on a fixed schedule at definite hours, in both heat and cold; you must not drink cold water nor can you have a drink of wine whenever you want. You must hand yourself over to your coach exactly as you would to a doctor. Then in the contest itself you must gouge and be gouged, there will be times when you will sprain a wrist, turn your ankle, swallow mouthfuls of sand, and be flogged. And after all that there are times when you lose.

Training

Olympic wrestlers usually trained in their home city-states for 9 months, although a select few were fortunate enough to be able to train in the city-state of Elis. They exercised in a large, open space called a gymnasium. A covered running track circled the open space. Usually there was a lake or river where athletes could swim. Attached to the gymnasium was the wrestling school, or *palaestra*. When the athletes trained—and later, when they competed in the Olympics—they did not wear clothes. They covered their bodies with sacred olive oil. It helped keep the athlete's skin from drying out and worked as a tanning lotion. After oiling their bodies, athletes in the contact sports dusted their bodies with sand or powder. This made it easier for their opponents to grip their bodies during competition.

Usually, wrestlers started their workouts with general exercises,

This carving comes from the base of an ancient Greek statue made during the sixth century B.C. It shows a Greek wrestler and his trainer.

such as stretches and weight lifting. The images on some ancient Greek vases tell us some athletes exercised to music. Once wrestlers finished their warm-ups, they practiced different wrestling moves, supervised by their trainers.

Style was very important. Wrestlers learned how to stand and balance correctly. They practiced throwing each other and also learned the proper way to be thrown. Wrestlers were expected to be strong, skillful, and graceful—all at the same time!

After 9 months of difficult training, it was time to register for the Olympics. Thirty days before the games started, athletes and their trainers went to Elis, where they signed up and continued training until the games began. During this training, athletes could withdraw if they thought the competition was too tough. But once the games started, they could no longer withdraw hon-

Olympic Appetites

Since there were age classes but no weight classes in ancient wrestling, smaller, lighter athletes couldn't compete well. Wrestlers ate as much as they could, hoping to get bigger and stronger than their opponents. The great wrestler Milo of Croton reportedly ate as much as 20 pounds (9 kg) of meat and 20 pounds (9 kg) of bread in a day. He drank up to $2\frac{1}{2}$ gallons (11 l) of wine. The most you might eat in a day is 1 pound ($\frac{1}{2}$ kg) of meat and about $\frac{1}{2}$ pound ($\frac{1}{4}$ kg) of bread. You might drink $\frac{1}{2}$ gallon ($2\frac{1}{4}$ l) of liquids. How does an ancient wrestler's food intake compare with yours?

One story tells about a wrestler named Astyanax of Miletus. He ate all the food at a party, leaving nothing for the other guests. When Astyanax died, his bones were too big to fit into the large jar normally used for burial. They took up two jars!

orably. Then, 2 days before the games began, wrestlers and other athletes, their families, judges, and trainers began the 40-mile procession from Elis to Olympia.

Wrestling in the Ancient Olympics

Imagine you're a spectator at the ancient Olympics. It's the fourth day, the time you've been waiting for. The contact sports, including wrestling, occur today. Two forms of wrestling take place. In upright wrestling, or *orthia pale*, the goal is to throw your opponent to the ground three times. In ground wrestling, or *kato pale*, opponents wrestle on the ground until one admits defeat. There are no breaks during either kind of wrestling.

The upright wrestling competition is about to begin. From the *altis*—the area with the sacred altars—you watch the huge, muscular competitors enter the sand pit, or *skamma*. Most have short hair so no one can pull it. A few wear leather caps.

The first two wrestlers push and shove, trying to force each other to the ground. However, they are not allowed to kick or hit. One wrestler uses a move called the "flying mare." He grabs the other wrestler's arm and throws him over his shoulder. Crash! The wrestler hits the ground. It's his third fall, and he loses. Defeated, he gets up and limps away.

The wrestling continues. One wrestler grips another in the "body hold." He grabs his opponent by the waist, lifts him off the ground, flips him in the air, and throws him to the ground. The

Wrestling in Greek Myths

- Some legends say that Herakles (Hercules) used the "flying mare" when he wrestled a lion during his first labor. He also wrestled a giant who needed to touch the earth to be strong. Herakles lifted the giant off the ground and killed him.
- Other legends tell about a wrestling match involving the hero Peleus. In ancient Greece, athletic games were conducted at funerals to honor the dead. At the funeral games for a dead king, Peleus wrestled a woman named Atalanta, who was a warrior and hunter. Peleus lost!

wrestler on the ground trips the other one. They both rise and continue the struggle. After more pushing, shoving, grunting, and sweating, one of them wins.

Finally, only two wrestlers remain. They fight fiercely until one is victorious and the other is defeated. You cheer the *triakter*, or winner, as the wrestlers leave the grounds.

The First Olympic Wrestling Champion

Although wrestling had a long history when the first ancient Olympics were held in 776 B.C., it did not become an Olympic sport until 708 B.C. Whoever won that year's wrestling competition would be the very first Olympic wrestling champion. The favorite was Eurybatus of Sparta. It's not surprising a Spartan would be favored. The city-state of Sparta placed great value on developing strong bodies, and training in wrestling began in childhood.

Eurybatus was large, with powerful arms and legs and bulging muscles. He easily defeated several opponents and reached the

The Rules of Upright Wrestling

Based on old writings and images on ancient Greek vases, we believe these were the rules of upright wrestling from the ancient Olympics.

- Holds had to be above the waist.
- One athlete had to throw the other onto the ground.
- The athlete who was thrown had to land on a hip, back, shoulder, or both knees for the throw to count.
- One wrestler had to throw the other one to the ground three times to win.
- The judges made the final decision about the throws.
- Biting, punching, and eye gouging were not allowed.
- Tripping was allowed.
- Breaking your opponent's fingers was allowed.
- Choking your opponent was allowed.

final match. The score was tied at two throws each when Eurybatus threw his opponent to the ground for a third time and won the first olive wreath for wrestling.

Other Great Achievements in Ancient Olympic Wrestling

Time has destroyed most ancient Olympic records. However, some information about remarkable wrestling accomplishments has come down to us. For example, the ancient Greek writer Pausanius recorded that Leontiskos was the Olympic wrestling champion three times in the fifth century B.C. Pausanius also reported that Leontiskos won by breaking his opponents' fingers! Of course, this would never be allowed in the modern Olympics.

A wrestler named Kleitomakhos remarkably managed to go through an entire competition without being thrown to the ground even once. How did people know this? He didn't have any sand sticking to his oily skin.

Pausanius also reported the astonishing achievement of the Spartan wrestler Hipposthenes. In 608 B.C., Hipposthenes won his sixth Olympic wrestling competition. This led the Spartans to worship him as a god and build a temple in his honor. Hipposthenes' son, Hetoemocles, won five Olympic wrestling championships.

Milo of Croton: Ancient Olympic Superstar

Milo of Croton—sometimes called Milo the Giant—was the most famous ancient wrestler. He came from the Greek colony of Croton in southern Italy. In 540 B.C., he won the Olympic boys' class. Eight years later, Milo won his first of five Olympic men's upright wrestling championships. Milo was so dominant that no other wrestlers would compete against him at one Olympics!

In 512 B.C., Timasitheus, a young man from Croton, broke Milo's winning streak. The agile Timasitheus simply kept out of the aging Milo's reach until Milo got tired and admitted defeat.

In addition to his Olympic victories, Milo won twenty-six other wrestling championships. He became a folk hero, and people told stories—probably exaggerated—about his strength and deeds.

One story told how Milo would tie a cord around his forehead and then expand veins in his head until they snapped the cord. Another story told about him walking around the Olympic stadium carrying a young bull across his shoulders. At the end of the games that day, he ate the entire bull for dinner. Yet another story tells how Milo held up a huge pillar of a collapsing building so others could escape. Of course, Milo also saved himself.

Think like a wrestler. What move might you make next? Are you in a position to flip your opponent? Could you trip him?

Early Heroes of Modern Olympic Wrestling

When the modern Olympics started in 1896, the organizers included wrestling. They liked its connection with the ancient games and used the style they believed ancient Greek athletes had used. This style became known as Greco-Roman wrestling. Wrestlers stood upright and used their arms and upper bodies. Holds below the waist were not allowed.

The 1904 Olympics didn't include Greco-Roman wrestling but introduced a style of wrestling called freestyle. In freestyle, wrestlers use their legs as well as their upper bodies. Lifting, pushing, tripping, and holding below the waist are allowed. Both forms of wrestling have been part of every Olympics since 1920.

Unlike the ancient Olympics, the modern Olympics groups wrestlers into weight classes. The number of classes has varied over time. In 1920, there were ten classes—five each in Greco-Roman and freestyle. By 1932, there were seven classes in each style.

Olympic Wrestling Weight Classes Then and Now

Weight limits for the different Olympic wrestling classes have also changed over time. This chart compares weight classes from 1936 with weight classes in 2004.

Class	Weight in 1936	Weight in 2004
Bantamweight	up to 123 pounds (56 kg)	up to 121 pounds (55 kg)
Featherweight	123–134 pounds (56–61 kg)	121–132 pounds (55–60 kg)
Lightweight	134–145 pounds (61–66 kg)	132–145 pounds (60–66 kg)
Welterweight	145–158 pounds (66–72 kg)	145–163 pounds (66–74 kg)
Middleweight	158–174 pounds (72–79 kg)	163–185 pounds (74–84 kg)
Light Heavyweight	174–191 pounds (79–87 kg)	not a class in 2004
Heavyweight	over 191 pounds (over 87 kg)	185–211 pounds (84–96 kg)
Super Heavyweight	not a class in 1936	211–264 pounds (96–120 kg)

An Introduction to Wrestling Rules

In the rest of this book, you'll read about some great moments in modern Olympic wrestling. But first, you need to learn a little bit about wrestling's rules and scoring.

- A competition is called a match or bout. An Olympic match today consists of one 5-minute period.

- Points are awarded for various moves during the match.

- A wrestler's aim is to pin the opponent or score the most points. A pin, or fall, occurs when a wrestler forces both of the opponent's shoulders onto the mat.

- As soon as one wrestler pins the other, the match is over.

- If neither wrestler pins the other, points determine the winner.

- A wrestler who leads a match by ten points wins. If neither wrestler has a ten-point lead, the one with the most points wins.

- A wrestler must score at least three points to win. If neither wrestler has three points, or in case of a tie, the match goes into sudden-death overtime. This lasts 3 minutes, or until one wrestler scores. If no points are scored, the judges decide the winner.

Wrestling at the First Modern Olympics, 1896

The 1896 Olympics in Athens, Greece, featured Greco-Roman wrestling. There were no weight classes or time limits. Matches were held outside, just as in the ancient Olympics. Five athletes from four countries took part. The two Greek wrestlers—Georgios

Tsitas and Stephanos Christopoulos—were the only ones who did not compete in other sports as well.

Many experts expected Great Britain's weight lifter Launceston Elliot to win. Greeks hoped one of their wrestlers would win. However, neither of these things happened. The man who became the first modern Olympic wrestling champion was a gymnast.

Carl Schuhmann: First Modern Olympic Champion

Carl Schuhmann was a member of the German gymnastics team, which won two gymnastics team competitions. Schuhmann also won an individual event. When he decided to compete in wrestling as well, it was considered unlikely he would win. After all, he was a gymnast, not a wrestler. He was also smaller and lighter than the other competitors. However, Schuhmann was a talented, agile athlete. In the first match, he defeated the favorite, weight-lifting champion Launceston Elliot. In the final match, he faced Greece's Georgios Tsitas. The men wrestled for 40 minutes, but neither won. Since it was dark by then, the match was halted and scheduled to continue the next day. When Schuhmann and Tsitas met again the next day, it took Schuhmann only about 15 minutes to defeat his rival. Thus the slight German gymnast became the first Olympic Greco-Roman wrestling champion. Tsitas finished second, and his fellow Greek, Stephanos Christopoulos, finished third.

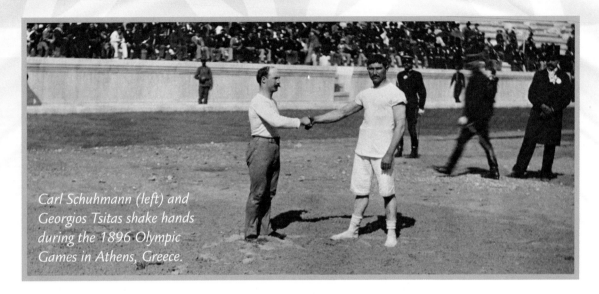

Carl Schuhmann (left) and Georgios Tsitas shake hands during the 1896 Olympic Games in Athens, Greece.

Freestyle Wrestling Becomes an Olympic Sport

Wrestling was not included in the 1900 games in Paris, France. The 1904 games in St. Louis, Missouri, didn't include Greco-Roman wrestling but did introduce a new type of wrestling commonly known as "catch as catch can." It didn't have the historical significance of Greco-Roman wrestling, but was immensely popular at fairs and festivals in the United States and Great Britain. It was introduced to the Olympics as freestyle wrestling.

The World's Longest Wrestling Match

The longest wrestling match on record occurred at the 1912 Olympics in Stockholm, Sweden. Russia's Martin Klein and Finland's Alfred Asikainen wrestled for 11 hours and 40 minutes in the Greco-Roman middleweight semifinals! Klein won, but was too tired to face Sweden's Claes Johanson in the finals. So Johanson won the gold medal, Klein took the silver medal, and Asikainen received the bronze.

In contrast to 1896, when there were no weight classes, there were seven weight classes in 1904.

In 1904, there were no airlines and few cars. St. Louis was hard to get to, especially for athletes from other countries. So most Olympic athletes came from the United States. In fact, all the wrestlers were American—so the United States won all the medals.

George Mehnert: First Modern Wrestling Superstar

George Mehnert was one of the most remarkable wrestlers in the 1904 games. Today he's considered the first superstar of modern amateur wrestling. Mehnert won the gold medal in the flyweight class. At that time, flyweight was for wrestlers weighing between 105 pounds (48 kg) and 115 pounds (52 kg). Although Mehnert was small, he was extremely talented. His victory should have come as no surprise. Mehnert was so good that many competitors refused to wrestle him. Between 1901 and 1908, Mehnert took part in fifty-nine matches in national tournaments and won all but one. In one victory, Mehnert pinned his opponent in only 7 seconds, a record that stood for many years.

Four years after his victory in St. Louis, Mehnert competed in the London Olympics. He was then a few pounds heavier and wrestled in the bantamweight class for athletes weighing between 115 pounds (52 kg) and 125 pounds (57 kg). Mehnert again won the gold medal, making him the first U.S. wrestler to win two

Olympic gold medals. No other American wrestler matched this feat until Bruce Baumgartner in 1992.

Great Wrestling Moments at the 1932 Olympics

The 1932 Olympics took place in Los Angeles, California. The Great Depression made it impossible for many foreign athletes to afford the long trip. Although only half as many athletes came to Los Angeles as had gone to Amsterdam, the Netherlands, in 1928, the quality of competition was high. Eighteen world records were equaled or broken.

Two remarkable achievements occurred in wrestling. Sweden's Carl Westergren became the first wrestler to win three gold medals. Another Swedish wrestler, Ivar Johansson, became the first wrestler to win gold medals in both Greco-Roman and freestyle at the same Olympics.

An Undefeated Olympic Champion

When U.S. wrestler Allie Roy Morrison arrived at the 1928 Olympics in Amsterdam, the Netherlands, he already had a remarkable record. He had lost only one match in high school and was so far undefeated in college. However, Morrison faced some tough opponents in the Olympic freestyle featherweight class.

Morrison defeated his first opponent, a Belgian wrestler, in two straight matches. He did the same with his next opponent, Finland's Kustaa Pihlajamäki, who had won the gold medal in the bantamweight class 4 years earlier. And he did it again with his next opponent, Switzerland's Hans Minder. Morrison won the gold medal without losing a single Olympic match! Sadly, he suffered a serious injury in a 1929 match that forced him to retire.

Carl Westergren

Carl Westergren was known for his intelligence, tactical skills, and concentration. He frightened his opponents before the match even began by rubbing the muscles in his arms and announcing, "Considering how strong I feel today, nobody can beat me!"

Westergren won many championships, but his first great victory came at the 1920 Olympics in Antwerp, Belgium. He won the gold medal in the middleweight class, for wrestlers weighing between 150 pounds (68 kg) and 165 pounds (75 kg). Four years later, at the games in Paris, France, Westergren won in the light heavyweight class, for wrestlers weighing between 165 pounds (75 kg) and 183 pounds (83 kg). At the 1928 Olympics in Amsterdam, Westergren gave up after an early loss to Finland's Onni Pellinen and won no medals. However, he returned to the 1932 Los Angeles games in the heavyweight class, for wrestlers weighing over 183 pounds (83 kg). Again, Westergren triumphed. With this victory, he became the first Olympic wrestler to win three gold medals.

Ivar Johansson

Ivar Johansson's accomplishment was even more spectacular than Westergren's. Johansson was the 1931 European Greco-Roman middleweight champion. However, he lost an Olympic qualifying match. As a result, he was placed in the lighter welterweight class.

However, he was allowed to compete in freestyle in the middleweight class. Thus he was in the unusual—some would say impossible—situation of competing in events in two different weight classes in the same Olympics.

The freestyle event was first. Johansson lost his first match but won the gold medal. Then he had to prepare for his Greco-Roman welterweight event the next day. Before each event, wrestlers had to weigh in to be sure their weight was within the required range. To pass the weigh-in, Johansson had to lose 16 pounds (7 kg) overnight. How could he do it? Immediately after the freestyle event, Johansson spent several hours in the sauna. By weigh-in time the next morning, he had sweated away all 16 pounds (7 kg)! However, this was only part of the battle. Losing that much weight so quickly is very hard on a person's body. Losing it by spending hours in a hot sauna puts additional strain on the body. No one today would advise doing that, as it could lead to serious health damage.

In spite of this, Johansson won the welterweight Greco-Roman event and became the first wrestler to win two gold medals at the same Olympics. At the 1936 games in Berlin, Germany, he became the second wrestler in history to win three gold medals when he won the middleweight Greco-Roman championship.

Kristjan Palusalu

At the 1936 Olympics in Berlin, Germany, Estonian wrestler Kristjan Palusalu repeated Ivar Johansson's accomplishment of winning gold medals in both freestyle and Greco-Roman. However, Palusalu won both his medals in the same weight class—heavyweight.

Estonian heavyweight wrestler Kristjan Palusalu appears here in a photo taken August 1, 1936, at the Berlin Olympics.

Modern Olympic Wrestling After World War II

World War II, which lasted from 1939 to 1945, interrupted the Olympics. No games were held in 1940 or 1944. The Olympics resumed in 1948, when they were held in London. That year, a new weight class was added to both freestyle and Greco-Roman, for a total of sixteen classes. The number of classes remained the same until 1972, when two classes were added to each style, for a total of twenty. The number of classes changed again after the 1996 games, when two weight classes were dropped from each style. The Athens games in 2004 saw the biggest change in Olympic wrestling history. For the first time, women's freestyle wrestling was an event. There were four classes of women's wrestling. Another weight class was dropped from both men's freestyle and Greco-Roman, leaving a total of fourteen men's wrestling classes.

A New Record in 1972

No wrestler won three gold medals again until 1972, when Soviet wrestler Aleksandr Medved won his third. Medved was also the first to win medals at three Olympics in a row. And he was the first freestyle wrestler to win three gold medals.

During the 1964 Olympic Games in Tokyo, Medved won his first gold medal in the freestyle light heavyweight division. In Mexico City 4 years later, he won his second gold medal, this time in the heavyweight division. By the time Medved got to the 1972 Olympics in Munich, Germany, he had moved up to the super heavyweight division. At about 260 pounds (118 kg), he was at the light end of this group. In fact, only one other wrestler in the class weighed less than he did. One of his opponents was Chris Taylor, who weighed about 412 pounds and was the heaviest Olympian ever. It seemed there was no way Medved could win the match. He used all his skills and drew on all his experience and managed to defeat Taylor. He also defeated his next opponent and once again won the gold medal. The International Federation of Amateur Wrestling (FILA) recognized Medved's achievement by naming him the Greatest Wrestler of the 20th Century in Freestyle.

After winning his third gold medal, Medved announced his retirement and kissed the wrestling mat. However, he wasn't entirely finished with the Olympics. At the 1980 games in Moscow, he administered the oath to the judges. Today, he is the Olympic freestyle wrestling coach for his home country of Belarus.

A Greco-Roman Record in 1996

Aleksandr Medved's freestyle wrestling achievement was duplicated by Greco-Roman wrestler Aleksandr Karelin at the 1996 games in Atlanta, Georgia. However, unlike Medved, Karelin won his three gold medals in the same weight class—super heavyweight. He was the first wrestler to do this.

Karelin, who weighed 286 pounds (130 kg), was sometimes called "King Kong" by his opponents. His first Olympic victory came at the

German heavyweight wrestler Wilfred Dietrich (on bottom) throws 412-pound (187-kg) Chris Taylor during a match at the 1972 Olympics in Munich, Germany.

The Most Olympic Wrestling Medals

Wilfried Dietrich of Germany holds the record for the most Olympic medals won in wrestling. Here's the list of his medals and his age when he won each.

- Silver, Greco-Roman Heavyweight, 1956; age 23
- Silver, Greco-Roman Heavyweight, 1960; age 26
- Gold, Freestyle Heavyweight, 1960; age 26
- Bronze, Greco-Roman Heavyweight, 1964; age 31
- Bronze, Freestyle Heavyweight, 1968; age 35

1988 games in Seoul, South Korea. Karelin easily won his first four matches, but his final match was a challenge. With 30 seconds to go, Karelin's opponent led by 3 points to 0. Then Karelin wrapped his arms around his opponent's waist, lifted him off the ground, and threw him feet first over his head. Karelin scored 5 points with this throw and won his first gold medal.

He easily won again at the 1992 games in Barcelona, Spain. Only one of his opponents made it to the end of the match. In Atlanta, Georgia, in 1996, Karelin went undefeated against all five opponents and won his third gold medal. When he got to the 2000 Olympics in Sydney, Australia, Karelin had been wresting for 13 years and had never lost in international competition! He hoped to win a fourth gold medal. However, he experienced a rare loss of concentration. The U.S.'s Rulon Gardner took advantage of this and defeated Karelin, winning the gold medal and ending Karelin's astounding winning streak. Karelin still won the silver medal. FILA recognized his amazing record by naming him the Greatest Wrestler of the 20th Century in Greco-Roman.

An Underdog's Victory in 2000

When Aleksandr Karelin faced Rulon Gardner in the final Greco-Roman super heavyweight match in Sydney, Australia, in 2000, no one could imagine what was about to happen. Gardner was the underdog. He had grown up on a Wyoming dairy farm. His best finish in international competition was fifth place. Karelin was undefeated in 13 years of international competition. Certainly he would defeat this farm boy. However, that's not what happened. Gardner forced the match into overtime. Then, with only 5 seconds to go, Karelin admitted defeat. Incredibly, the Wyoming farm boy had defeated the greatest Greco-Roman wrestler of the twentieth century and won the gold medal! Overcome with emotion, Gardner did a cartwheel and a somersault, then ran a victory lap around the arena. It was an unforgettable moment for athletes and spectators alike.

Rulon Gardner: Injuries and Triumph in 2004

As amazing as Gardner's victory was, the next part of his story was even more remarkable. Gardner faced great personal challenges between the 2000 Olympics and the 2004 Olympics in Athens, Greece. In 2002, he became lost riding a snowmobile in temperatures below 0°F (−18°C). He was rescued, but the extreme cold injured one toe so badly it had to be amputated. He had little feeling left in his other toes. It took Gardner a full year to recover. Then, in March 2004, he was injured in a motorcycle accident.

An American Champion

At the 1992 Olympics in Barcelona, Spain, super heavyweight freestyle wrestler Bruce Baumgartner became the first American wrestler to win medals at three Olympics in a row. He won gold medals in 1984 and 1992, and a silver medal in 1988. He won a fourth medal—a bronze—at the 1996 games in Atlanta, Georgia. Only seven other American athletes have earned medals in four different Olympics.

At the 2000 Olympics in Sydney, Australia, Rulon Gardner (on the right) won an unexpected victory over Aleksandr Karelin.

That was followed by a wrist injury in May that required surgery.

In spite of these injuries, Gardner made the 2004 Olympic team. He didn't win the gold medal in Athens, but Gardner was happy to win the bronze medal. It was an awesome achievement for someone with little feeling in his toes and several pins in one wrist.

Gardner knew it was time to retire. At the end of the match, he put his wrestling shoes in the center of the mat. His brother, also a wrestler, explained this was an ancient ritual—Gardner was paying tribute to the wrestling gods. It was an emotional moment for Gardner, his family, and fans. Gardner later wrote that winning the 2004 bronze medal was a moment of great pride, given what he had to overcome to reach the Olympics at all. It is an inspiring story that represents the Olympic spirit at its best.

Olympic Wrestling

A South Korean Champion

At the 2000 Olympics in Sydney, Australia, Kwon-Ho Sim became the first South Korean man to win two gold medals in the Summer Olympics. He had won in the Greco-Roman light flyweight class at the 1996 Atlanta, Georgia, games. He was slightly heavier by the time of the Sydney games, so his victory there was in the flyweight class.

A New Chapter in Olympic Wrestling

The 2004 Olympics in Athens, Greece, introduced something new and exciting. For the first time, the games included women's freestyle wrestling. There were four weight classes. Fifty women from twenty countries competed. All these women hold a special place in Olympic history. Those who won medals have the additional honor of being the first to do so in women's Olympic wrestling.

The competitions took place in weight-class order, starting with the lightest class. Japan's dominant team expected to win all the gold medals. However, that's not how it turned out.

History will remember Ukrainian Irini Merleni as the first woman to win an Olympic

At the 2004 Olympics in Athens, Greece, a tearful Rulon Gardner clutches a U.S. flag as he walks off the mat. He has followed Olympic tradition by leaving his shoes in the center of the mat to announce his retirement.

wrestling gold medal. She also had the best record of all winners in all weight classes. It took Merleni only 4 minutes 36 seconds to defeat her three first opponents! None of those opponents scored any points. Her opponent in the semifinals—Patricia Miranda of the United States—couldn't score any points either. In the finals, Merleni faced Japan's Chiharu Icho, the reigning world champion in a higher weight class and the favorite at the Olympics. With only $2\frac{1}{2}$ minutes left in their match, Icho was ahead. Then Merleni tied the score. When the match ended, the judges declared Merleni the winner! Chiharu Icho won the silver medal, and Miranda took the bronze. Japanese fans were disappointed, but there were still three gold medals to be won.

In the next weight class—106 to 121 pounds (48 to 55 kg)—Japan's Saori Yoshida defeated her first two opponents without either of them scoring any points. Yoshida faced a tougher opponent in the semifinals. She won the match, but just barely. In the finals, Yoshida again prevented her opponent from scoring any points. Japan had its first gold medal in women's wrestling. Canada's Tonya Verbeek won the silver medal, and France's Anna Gomis received the bronze.

Chiharu Icho's sister, Kaori, was favored to win in the next weight class—121 to 139 pounds (55 to 63 kg). She easily defeated her first two opponents. However, like Yoshida, Kaori faced a much tougher opponent in the semifinals. She won, but just barely. In the finals,

Kaori Icho faced another tough opponent, American Sara McMann. McMann controlled the first two-thirds of the match, and it looked as if Japan might be upset again. However, Kaori Icho finally scored points. She won the match, and Japan had its second gold medal. Sara McMann took the silver medal, and France's Lise Legrand won the bronze.

In the heaviest weight class, the favorite was once again a Japanese wrestler, Kyoko Hamaguchi. Her father was a professional wrestler, and they had trained together for many years. Hamaguchi had already won five World Championships. She won her first two matches fairly easily. In the semifinals, she faced China's Wang Xu, an 18-year-old with little experience. Even Wang expected Hamaguchi to win. However, to everyone's amazement, Wang defeated Hamaguchi and went

Irini Merleni (in blue) and Chiharu Icho are locked in combat during the finals at the 2004 Olympics in Athens, Greece.

Women's Weight Classes

- up to 106 pounds (48 kg)
- 106 to 121 pounds (48 to 55 kg)
- 121 to 139 pounds (55 to 63 kg)
- 139 to 159 pounds (63 to 72 kg)

on to win the gold medal! Russia's Gouzel Maniourova won the silver medal, and Hamaguchi had to settle for bronze. China has not produced many Olympic medalists in wrestling, but perhaps Wang Xu is evidence of great things yet to come.

Timeline

776 B.C.	Olympia, Greece. The first recorded ancient Olympic games are held.
708 B.C.	Olympia, Greece. Wrestling is added to the ancient Olympics. Eurybatus becomes the first Olympic wrestling champion.
608 B.C.	Olympia, Greece. Hipposthenes wins men's Olympic wrestling for the sixth time. His fellow Spartans worship him as a god.
540 B.C.	Olympia, Greece. Milo of Croton wins boys' Olympic wrestling.
516 B.C.	Olympia, Greece. Milo of Croton wins men's Olympic wrestling for the fifth time.
512 B.C.	Olympia, Greece. Timasitheus breaks Milo's winning streak.
A.D. 393	Roman emperor Theodosius I ends the Olympics.
1896	Athens, Greece. First modern Olympics are held. German gymnast Carl Schuhmann wins the first Olympic gold medal for wrestling.
1904	St. Louis, Missouri. Freestyle wrestling is added to the Olympics. George Mehnert wins the gold medal for freestyle wrestling.
1908	London, United Kingdom. Mehnert becomes the first U.S. wrestler to win a second Olympic gold medal.
1932	Los Angeles, California. Swedish Greco-Roman wrestler Carl Westergren becomes the first man to win three gold medals in wrestling. Swedish wrestler Ivar Johansson wins gold medals as a welterweight in Greco-Roman and as a middleweight in freestyle. He's the first to win gold medals in both at the same Olympics.
1936	Berlin, Germany. Ivar Johansson becomes the second wrestler in history to win three gold medals.
1964	Tokyo, Japan. German wrestler Wilfried Dietrich wins his fifth gold medal. No other wrestler has won so many. Soviet freestyle wrestler Aleksandr Medved wins his first gold medal.
1972	Munich, Germany. Medved becomes the first wrestler to win gold medals at three Olympics in a row. He also becomes the first freestyle wrestler to win three gold medals.
1996	Atlanta, Georgia. Soviet wrestler Aleksandr Karelin becomes the first Greco-Roman wrestler to win gold medals at three Olympics in a row. He is also the first wrestler to win all his gold medals in the same weight class. U.S. freestyle wrestler Bruce Baumgartner becomes the eighth U.S. athlete to win medals in four Olympics.
2000	Sydney, Australia. U.S. Greco-Roman wrestler Rulon Gardner defeats Karelin to win the gold medal. Kwon-Ho Sim becomes the first South Korean athlete to win two gold medals in the Summer Olympics.
2004	Athens, Greece. Women's freestyle wrestling is introduced, with four weight classes. Irina Merleni of the Ukraine is the first woman to win an Olympic gold medal for wrestling. Rulon Gardner comes back after numerous injuries and wins the bronze medal in Greco-Roman.

Glossary

altis The area at ancient Olympia that had the sacred altars.

amputate To cut off or remove, especially the removal of a limb by surgery.

archaeologist Someone who studies the remains of peoples from the past to understand how they lived.

city-state An independent state made up of a city and its surrounding areas.

contact sport A sport that requires contact with the opponent's body. Wrestling is a contact sport. Running is not a contact sport.

discus A circular disk that is thrown.

flog To beat with a rod or whip.

freeborn Not born into slavery; born as a free person.

Great Depression A period of history during the late 1920s and 1930s. Banks and businesses lost money, and there were few jobs.

Greco-Roman A style of wrestling based on the practices of ancient Greece and Rome.

historian Someone who studies the past.

hold One of several particular ways of grasping an opponent in wrestling.

javelin A light spear that is thrown for distance in competition.

labor One of twelve tasks the gods assigned to Herakles as punishment.

overtime Extra time beyond a set limit.

pagan Having to do with the religious systems of ancient Greece and Rome, which involved belief in more than one god.

sauna A bathhouse which is filled with steam by throwing water on hot stones.

semifinals An event held in a contest to see if a person can go on to the final event.

Soviet Having to do with the former Soviet Union. The Soviet Union was made up of fifteen countries, including Russia.

sudden-death An overtime in a sporting event that does not have a fixed time limit. It ends when one team scores.

summer solstice The longest day of the year and the first day of summer.

tactical Skilled in planning and carrying out the moves necessary to achieve a goal.

underdog The one expected to lose a competition.

For More Information

International Olympic Committee
Château de Vidy
1007 Lausanne
Switzerland
Phone: 41-21-621-61-11
Web site: www.olympic.org

USA Wrestling
6155 Lehman Drive
Colorado Springs, CO 80918
Phone: (719) 598-8181
Web site: www.themat.com

U.S. Olympic Training Center–Colorado Springs National Headquarters
Olympic House
One Olympic Plaza
Colorado Springs, CO 80909-5760
Phone: (719) 632-5551
Web site: www.olympic-usa.org

Web Sites

Due to the changing nature of Internet links, the Rosen Publishing Group, Inc., has developed an online list of Web sites related to the subject of this book. This site is updated regularly. Please use this link to access the list: **http://www.rosenlinks.com/gmoh/wres**

For Further Reading

Gifford, Clive. *Summer Olympics: The Definitive Guide to the World's Greatest Sports Celebration.* Boston, MA: Kingfisher, 2004.

Swaddling, Judith. *The Ancient Olympic Games.* Austin, TX: University of Texas Press, 2000.

U.S. Olympic Committee. *Olympism: A Basic Guide to the History, Ideals, and Sports of the Olympic Movement.* Milwaukee, WI: Gareth Stevens Publishing, 2001.

Young, David C. *A Brief History of the Olympic Games.* Malden, MA: Blackwell Publishing, 2004.

Bibliography

Associated Press. "Japan Wins Two Gold Medals." ESPN Online. August 24, 2004. Retrieved September 2006 (http://sports.espn.go.com/oly/summer04/wrestling/news/story?id=1865521).

Collins Gerry. "Kyoko Hamaguchi: Five-Star Champion." *ABC News Online.* Retrieved September 2006 (http://abc.net.au/olympics/2004/profiles/kyokohamaguchi.htm).

Gardner, Rulon, with Bob Schaller. *Never Stop Pushing: My Life from a Wyoming Farm to the Olympic Medals Stand.* New York: Carroll & Graf Publishers, 2005.

Glubok, Shirley, and Alfred Tamarin. *Olympic Games in Ancient Greece.* New York: Harper and Row, 1975.

Guinness World Records. "Most Olympic Wrestling Medals." Retrieved September 2006 (http://www.guinnessworldrecords.com/content_pages/record.asp?recordid=44191).
HickokSports.com. "Women's Freestyle Wrestling." Retrieved September 2006 (http://www.hickoksports.com/history/olwrestfw.shtml).
International Wrestling Hall of Fame. "Hall of Honors: Aleksandr Karelin." Retrieved September 2006 (http://www.filahalloffame.com/karelin.html).
International Wrestling Hall of Fame. "Hall of Honors: Carl Westergren." Retrieved September 2006 (http://www.filahalloffame.com/westergren.html).
Middleton, Haydn. *Ancient Olympic Games.* Chicago, IL: Heinemann Library, 2000.
National Wrestling Hall of Fame and Museum. "Distinguished Member: George Mehnert, Class of 1976." Retrieved September 24, 2006 (http://www.wrestlinghalloffame.org/awards/?dm&honoree=9).
Perrottet, Tony. *The Naked Olympics: The True Story of the Ancient Games.* New York: Random House, 2004.
U.S. Olympic Committee. *Olympism: A Basic Guide to the History, Ideals, and Sports of the Olympic Movement.* Milwaukee, WI: Gareth Stevens Publishing, 2001.
Wikipedia. "Wrestling at the 1896 Summer Olympics." Retrieved September 24, 2006 (http://en.wikipedia.org/wiki/Wrestling_at_the_1896_Summer_Olympics).
Woff, Richard. *The Ancient Greek Olympics.* New York: Oxford University Press, 1999.
www.olympic.org. "Carl Schuhmann: Champion of Both Gymnastics and Wrestling." Retrieved August 28, 2006 (http://www.olympic.org/uk/athletes/profiles/bio_uk.asp?PAR_I_ID=58111).
www.olympic.org. "Wrestling: Olympic Sport Since 1896." Retrieved August 26, 2006 (http://www.olympic.org/uk/sports/programme/index_uk.asp?SportCode=WR).

Index

About the Author

Barbara Linde has worked in education for over 30 years as an elementary school teacher and reading specialist, and as a university professor. For about the last 20 years, she has also been a writer and editor of educational materials. She has written more than twenty-five nonfiction books and a Virginia History textbook. Barbara lives in Yorktown, Virginia, with her husband and son. In her spare time, she enjoys dancing, swimming, traveling, quilting, and reading.

Photo Credits

Cover, pp. 8, 9, 12, 28, 33, 36, 39, 40, 42 © Getty Images; p. 7 © Shutterstock; p. 14 © Michael Nicholson/Corbis; p. 17 © B.S.P.I./Corbis; p. 23 © The Art Archive/Corbis.

Designer: Michael J. Flynn
Editor: Janey Levy